aetherius

Richard Jinghao Min

BookLeaf Publishing

Presentation by *BookLeaf Publishing*

Web: www.bookleafpub.com

E-mail: info@bookleafpub.com

ISBN: 9789357445351

First edition 2021

DEDICATION

To Aurora Fox, for traveling a thousand worlds with me

Praeludium

We were in a narrow cave
A point of light in the distance
Our arms tightly linked and trembling
As we stepped towards its glow

Reality seemed moments ago
But the whispering darkness came
She and I soon still arrived
At the end of a barren road

There exists a place so set in stone
Its unwavering beauty just as alone
Not life nor death, nor anything between
The island of amnesic dreams,

Openings, Arrivals

A night without its familiar glow
Without comfort nor warmth
Yet vivacious and hopeful
Upon a belated journey's end

I watched from afar
With snowy coats and starry eyes
Of the Harbinger's lucid return
Reflected in a hundred wishful hearts

A land without its everlasting ice
Without order nor refuge
Yet fractured in unity
Upon her undue leave

The worlds all but heralded
One celestial arrival
All but welcomed
One opening tempest

I lay dormant amongst the brush,
Watchful gaze sweeping the ridge
Snow-flecked furs fluttering
Thin arms tucked close within

Beyond the groves, the girl crept forth
I stood silently, just as unaware
Yet we met nonetheless in an embrace,

The Clan

A thousand lights shine upon its ripples
A thousand lights shine back unto the heavens
Blazing thunder echoes through
The silver primordial artery
A glistening flow winding through
The fertile subconscious valley

A hundred tribesmen followed her departure
A hundred tribesmen lavished her return
Sharp tunes and enchanted strums drift about
The rejoicing village
An effervescent harmony falls upon
The place we call home

Eight restored, time ephemeral
Serenity will shatter and we will notice
The snow's impurity

Arms linked with skyward souls
The boy and the girl returned
To the village so away from reality
Surrounded with others so truly alone
A Harbinger's return, a joyous light
A flame amid the Land of Ice

Tumbling drums awoke her slumber
Flaring horns disturbed my rest
The Tempest retrieved its olden glory
As her violet glance pierced the crowd
A frosted haze enveloped my soul
In an unmoving clash of violet and gold,

First Ascension

"We have met," she so firmly spoke
In a perturbed delay, her eyes faraway
Unsensing, unendearing, and ever unseeing

She stepped forward, blocking my voice
As what had been clouded faded away
I recalled the cries of tomorrow
Unwavering, unsparing, and ever unknowing

"Should this be real?" I whispered aloud
Spells splintering into oblivion
"Afraid so, afraid not," she smiled back
A worldly resonance in empty reflection
Undying, unbinding, and ever unloving

The thaw arrived before my wake
Cleansing the world in a feigned state
All stories and tales ebbed by fate
To the one above in this first ascension
A simpler plane of urbane desire
Unenlighetining and ever unapologizing

Mere hours within our fantasy
Minutes in reality
Seconds in perception

Fostering years in a single trance
Decades in solitude
Centuries in eudaemonia

Awake, awake, in cruel agony
In an alternate realm, an alternate dream,

Icarus

One blink, two sighs
Three worlds, four skies
Wings in flight and changing time
Casting shadows over tainted light

Frigid memories once more degrade
Of ice and flame, of returning fame
I have traversed beyond the old
Beyond broken bones and liquid gold

Five births, six deaths
Seven stars, eight nights
Above written destiny and crafted life
In my search for unbounded truth

In actuality, over splendid waves
Where the ebonite cosmos knows all
Freedom wails in its goodwill
To retreat to pleasures beneath

I lay now, above cloud nine
In the tenth ring from inside
For this place beyond the sky
In its perpetual orbital glide

In the central tower, a disorderly room
Where the snow had never fallen
Where villages were long lost relics
Where the only arterial rivers are ones above
I reawaken

Treading over the auroras
Falling across the heavens
Burning away the remnants of a once celestial
aria,

Syzygy

Once it left, it left for good
For better or for worse
For joy or for misery
All I recall is its disperse
So now here I watch, among the stars
In a luminous city, an era apart

Dazzling vibrance within the void
Majestic convergence in open pathways
Home of millions and bane of none
The Elysian fields and paradise

Once upon a faraway Earth
Rested a station of similar state
Yet it remains a singular speck
In the presence of the Icarus nest

I peer outside the crystalline glass
To watch a scarlet sphere appear
Across boundless horizons and wavering rays
For the cycle of rebirth every year

Beyond the street, the girl crept forth
I stood silently, still as unaware
But she halted before reaching near

And cried out a desperate warning

"Watch the sun!" her voice rang clear
As the crimson shine expanded away
Another golden orb and azure dome
Came into sight in an infernal sway
Three converged to intertwine
Destroying all as stars align,

Violet Flame

"We have met," she so firmly spoke
In a perturbed delay, her eyes faraway
Unsensing, unendearing, and ever unseeing

"Again?" I ask, glaring back
As flames engulfed the dying world
Her violet gaze saw no emotion
For she sensed and saw all within

"First a village and then a city
Yet I once again cannot discern
Where that boundary sets itself
Where illusion starts and real adjourns"

"Should this be real?" I spoke aloud
As the stars began to separate
"Why ask if you know?" she turned away
Leaving remnants of the present's past decay

I float alone in the vast emptiness
As familiar warmth seeps in my veins
An interlude for the ever sweet rain

For a single instant, I felt
The kiss of the snowy dawn

A clan's heartbeat in the cold

For a single instant, I felt
The shine of entrancing starlight
A metropolis once grandiose

Awake, awake, in cruel agony
In an alternate realm, an alternate dream,

Sapphire Bloom

A piercing blue at my first sight
Of a new oasis beside the waves
The darkness vanishing before my eyes
As they absently peer into the clouds

No longer in fiery celestial ruins
No longer with bitter glacial cliffs
I was brought out again to this retreat
To bright scents and summery sweets

What use were memories anyway?
Those troubled pasts were faraway
The time is now, the end is nigh
To break free from night and purify

A wayward breeze swept through the seas
Stirring beaches and bending trees
As ferries dock and sailboats drift
Gulls cry and scour for scattered gifts

I sense around in paramount joy
Unmoving yet so gleefully free
Hoping for a recognizable face
Within the flowing facade of time

She remained hidden for a while
Til' the golden fall and silver rise
For she knew I could not recall a name
That was once so pure and effortless
But now realms below the current frame
Below starry infernos, below barren valleys
In the unknowing depths of a space between
worlds,

Outlanders

Scarf wrapped around her blonde locks
The girl crept forth, desperate to triumph
As the ocean threatened to drag me under

Third time a charm, a final alarm
As she reached me once more and offered her
hand
Paralysis broke and I arose

As shadowy tides pulled away
Her golden gaze reached out to mine
Striking a deafening knell

The low-toned ring shattered the dark
Yielding the immediate light of day
I gripped her hand and pulled her close
Familiarity sang in a heartfelt cry
A brother's affection for this rejoin
An aching absence to subside

Together, we traverse the sands
Toward the twinkling complex beyond the rift
Skywards structures slowly shifting
As we step closer to its inner core
Her expectant watch and jubilant beam

Bringing life to this land and to me

Yet she abruptly stopped and carefully spoke
“Fate has arrived, we’ll meet again”
As the ocean rose, a blooming violet
To greet the outlanders it hated most,

The Harbinger

"We have met," she so firmly spoke
In a perturbed delay, her eyes faraway
Unsensing, unendearing, and ever unseeing

I turned around to my sibling's figure
Already fading in the fervent glow
Heart racing, my hands reach out
Only to grasp the luminescent emptiness

Anger brimmed with each passing second
Despair clouded up my sight
All delight drew into an abyss
Yet she remains ever nonchalant
I rest atop her extended palm
Ferociously calm but petrified
A distant gaze absorbs the land
While silent steps stir up the sea

"Should this be real?" I painfully pleaded
Coasts and cliffs parting aside
There was no response, no answer this time
But rather a brisk fling into the sky
Her serene complexion yielded no sign
No emotion nor reason, and strangely divine
As I reached higher, she let loose a sigh

"It has never been real, yet you denied"

"You were never the type of man to doubt
How and why you ever arrived
Only to be tortured once more and soon cast out
Can you see the past you have never derived"

Awake, awake, in cruel agony
In an alternate realm, an alternate dream,

Waters of Acheron

The mist dispersed into silent ripples
A single oar lay afloat the surface
The wishful boat in a steadfast river
Of tranquility and inconceivable woes
Saccharine drops fall from above
A sign of obscurity and painful love
Her aurelian gaze etched in my heart
Its memory a hundred lives apart

As the gentle current brings me away
The dreary banks a blank display
All sense of time ground to a halt
In place for heavy guilt and stifling fault
I raise my head to see star-strewn tarps
Promising the end to desire, to lust and greed
Yet the silken waters beneath so speak
Of a darker truth it so foresees

For one millennium
I so wandered this home
Of endless dreams and solitude
Seeking her shadow for an unknown goal
I traveled in flames, in ice, from seas to skies
Incomplete without her life

Around me rose a thousand souls
Pensive in their destined ordeals
Some accept their fate and laugh
Others struggle against its unshakable clasp
But we were one along the stream
The river of pain and the unredeemed,

Reservoir

A fortnight passed on the narrow raft
As the waters churned with swift updrafts
No sight to behold or chaotic unfold
An eternal song in a repeated echo

I am conscious in a pacific field
The ethereal glow amid lifeless flows
The remaining hope amid dying wills
A blazing soul amid the withering old

The Harbinger's words struck a spark
However small yet dispelling dark
I was never the type of man to doubt
How and why I ever arrived
Only to be tortured once more and soon cast out
Unseeing of the past I have never derived

Epochs change in the guise of time
My arrival seemed far in antiquity
Only illusions remain of that arcane day
When my eyes never opened again

Slowly but surely the reflection grew clear
Not in a month nor even a year

I resided within the emptiness of connected minds
A bottomless slumber where all is confined

Her aurelian gaze etched once more in my heart
Its memory closer than ever before
She arrived with me at this middle place
Before the Great After and its transcendent gates,

An Open End

The river slowed and I returned
To ancient arrivals and restless waves
A memory long forgotten but now obtained
From our beginnings in the unlit cave
We saw the lights as I do now
A limitless expanse of fading night
I made my final deathbound vow
To protect her from this afterlife

Yet now I see her silhouette
Among the ascended in the stars
But I cling onto whatever bet
Of seeing her before we depart
In all the worlds I have so tread
Her presence signaled an untimely close
And when we met on that midnight coast
I was torn away and ever morose

From the glowing sun, the figure appeared
To witness the end of the river's bound
The Harbinger came so enchantingly austere
Her cloak flowing and her head crowned
"We have met," I spoke before she began
In a perturbed delay, my eyes dismayed
A welcoming laugh pierced through the wind

As she knew I had my final say

Before another word would be uttered
All who remained rose out of the sea
Transcending our plane to seek another
Of glory or despair, suppressed or free
Awake, awake, in cruel agony
In an alternate realm, an alternate dream,

Where All Worlds Meet

"You have seen what was to be seen
You have learned what was to be learned
Yet you remain on this open sea
Heart awake and mind adrift
Tell me, traveler of afar
What do you seek in this lonely grave?"

"To see her again before we part
To hold her close and not let go

From the ice-born clan upon the ridge
From the destruction by starstruck blaze
From the wishful gales and city core
From the winding river that met its end

I remember her from a distant life
Brother and sister in a simpler time
But on that day we left our world
For this"

The Harbinger was all but gone
Leaving a single black rose above my boat

Where hundreds once were only I was left
So I reached for the petals in wretched hope
A tremble of pain spread through my bones
As I was lifted into the skies above

My veins ablaze with anguish
My vision clouded with dazzling radiance
She had sent me to the Great After
To end this journey where all worlds meet,

In Oblivion

There exists a place so set in stone
Its unwavering beauty just as alone
Not life nor death, nor anything between
The island of amnesic dreams

A mirage of peace unknowingly burst
As I arrived from sapphire plains below
My spirit ablaze in ecstasy
Scorching the soundless eternity

Amid blinding auras she softly slept
A shining beacon of tranquil life
Before I moved, her golden gaze
Lit up the clouds in a million rays

On light and dark within this space
Rest uncountable worlds of mystery
I knew not its purpose nor why I came
Just that I called out her forgotten name

For we were twins before our plight
And now united above hidden heavens
Where the sun shines in turbulent storms
Where day and night are equivalent forms

An existence not in reality nor dream
Where even those who passed could not see
If we were no more we would've long since
gone
Engulfed by the river instead of sailing on

Yet between her silken tears and my warming
words
We knew that time was limited
But we swore in our delirium
To stay forever in this oblivion,

Transcending

Once united we would never split
Together in a land after centuries apart
She remained at my side, a flair of life
A partner in crime and a dearest guide

Oblivion brought euphoric drive
Devoid of fear or painful strain
The blissful ignorance of a merry delusion
Yet it still was our paradise, our unbreakable will

No longer did time serve its role
For there was none within this home
In our daring and limitless curiosity
We set on a voyage across a hundred worlds

A hidden forest, a burning tower
A frozen ocean and a hall of power
Behind every door lay an unseen lore
A reason for our journeys and evermore

I could sense within mountainous peaks
By the largest of cities and on the ocean breeze
That violet gaze, ever aware
Of our blossoming dread flowing in the air

A sister's tears behind brimming smiles
Knowing our path will terminate
That every day we wake in this barren land
Fate could mark our last farewell,

Dusk

"How long has it been?"
Her voice rang out across golden meadows
Cast aglow by the setting sun
In an iridescent field of fire

"We have run since dawn, through seven worlds
Across a dozen seas, over a hundred hills
Should we not rest? For the day grows old
And the flowers will wither in the cold"

"Not now, dear sister, we must return
We will arrive soon, I promise you"

My pulse rising as she glanced my way
In the past few days her presence grew faint
All but a sliver of her light remains
She cannot worry and cannot know
But I fear for the worst as Fate comes near
Her eyes protested as she soon caught up
A fading form barely clinging on
I dried my sorrow and held her tight
As the evening glow birthed the night

"Are we still alive?"

I closed my eyes in a silent plea
For all these years within this cave
I had wondered the very same

Beneath the aging dusk
A lone man silently stood
Counting the seconds
Before her untimely end,

Great After

His umbral figure blocked our path
At the boundary line between foreign skies
A crimson gaze and outstretched hand
Reaching towards her indistinct form

An ornate scythe in his ivory fist
His somber complexion unchanging
Overbearing agony weighed upon me
As the moment arrived to be left behind

The celestial dome that was once serene
Shattered in place of a brilliant gleam
Her eyes widened at the glorious sight
And I let loose a despairing cry

"Her time is nigh, dear traveler
Even our Harbinger warned you so
Yet you cannot accept this destiny
That her river ends while your's still
flow"

"Perhaps instinct was always right
She seemed ever distant since that seaside night
I wanted just a shred of hope
But she already left me long ago"

I stared blankly at her by my side
A mere fragment of her former self
The last of her will to stay with me
Before Fate had chosen to set her free
With a final smile, she wiped my eyes
Death grasped her hand and ignored my cries

"We will meet soon," she called above
Her twinkling gaze ever full of love,

Everfrost

I am alone in this lifeless place
On a journey continued after aching loss
Returning to the land of oblivion
In a path that none will ever cross
The iceborn storm and its stinging rage
Froze the misery in my blood
For he was right about my fear
Of Fate and her overseer

As my steps grew soft and vigor drained
The familiar winged figure appeared again
Violet light cast upon the snow
Our Harbinger of tomorrow

"We have not yet met," she so firmly spoke
In a perturbed delay, her eyes faraway
Unsensing, unendearing, and ever unseeing

I managed a laugh beyond the strain
For her antics no longer had my care
We were all too familiar with what she had
caused
A song of life and death and all that's unfair

"This is the beginning of your tale

Of victory and loss, of pleasure and pain
As you are cursed to repeat for eternity
Within your own mind and own domain
I cannot help break this suffering
But I will be within every world
To keep you well alive and safe
And seek for the day you may awake"

In cruel agony or kind delight
For my days are numbered and worlds finite,

Endings, Departures

A night without its familiar glow
Without comfort nor warmth
Yet vivacious and hopeful
Upon a belated journey's end

I watched from afar
With snowy coats and starry eyes
Of the Harbinger's lucid return
Reflected in a hundred wishful hearts

This secluded space of years so yonder
Of closing chorales and sunken saints
Left me in the void to judge and ponder
For the cycle of torment devoid of gains
Deprived of grief and all that's dear
Beyond memory lane and delusional heed
Yet when all hope was lost she still appeared
The final strength to have me freed

Once an arrival so far apart
The desolate clan opening skyward dimensions
Of burning wings and orbiting stars
Of sapphire blooms and frantic ascensions
A reunited joy to be broken so soon
Towards riverside odes and wishful dreams

Until only I was left under a silvery moon
Thrown into oblivion and Fate's cruel seams

In these last hours, these ending scenes
I see her in the coming dawn
We are but one cosmos away
Forever together in night and day
A blinding light sends me awake
The end of an odyssey in this lifeless cave,

Postludium

On that warm, overcast afternoon
My lingering miserable trance no more
A delicate sheet draped over her bed
As the autumn breeze whistled

There exists a place so prone to change
Its unwavering simplicity is just as strange
Of life and death, and everything between
The ocean of reality

Awake, awake, in cruel agony
In a final realm, a final dream.

www.ingramcontent.com/pod-product-compliance
Lightning Source LLC
Chambersburg PA
CBHW051745130826
49812CB00033B/1017
9789357445351